St. Paul of the Cross

by Fr Ben Lodge C.P.

alive Publishing

First published in 2019 by Alive Publishing Ltd
Graphic House, 124 City Road, Stoke on Trent, ST4 2PH
Tel: +44 (0) 1782 745600 • Fax: +44 (0) 1782 745500
www.alivepublishing.co.uk • email: booksales@alivepublishing.co.uk

 British Library Catalogue-in-Publication Data.
A catalogue record for this book is available from the British Library.

ISBN: 978-1-906278-34-2

This pamphlet has been produced to mark the founding of the Passionist Order three hundred years ago by St. Paul of the Cross. It draws heavily on the book "As a seal upon your heart" by Fr. Paul Francis Spencer C.P. published by St. Paul's.

Cover image: courtesy of The Postulator.

CONTENTS

INTRODUCTION

To read the life of a person who lived three hundred years ago is very different from reading the life of someone who lived thirty years ago. The challenge is even greater if a different culture and language are involved. Ways of thinking and expressing ideas have radically changed. The ideas associated with human and individual rights had not been considered three hundred years ago. Even the way people think about, and relate to, God has fundamentally changed. But these differences do not mean that the life was wrong or without value. Rather it means that we have to work our way through the historical context and cultural differences to find what was essential in the life of the individual. When the individual concerned was also a mystic, the challenge of reading the life is considerably increased, for the fact is that mystical experiences are not that familiar for most of us, but again this does not take away from their validity.

Crucial in the life of any individual is their faith in God and their willingness to persevere in that faith, no matter what obstacles and sufferings they encounter along the way.

Within a couple of hundred feet of where St. Gregory the Great (540-604) sent St. Augustine to England, stands the church of Saints John and Paul, from where a second wave of missioners were sent from Italy to convert the English. Today this church is in the care of the Passionists, who have an extraordinary relationship with the English Church mainly due to the apostolate of St. Paul of the Cross, a little known Italian Saint who has had a huge influence on the development of the Catholic Church in England.

CHAPTER 1

BEGINNINGS

Paul Danei had never seen England; he didn't expect to, and he never did. He knew very little about England, this small island, far to the North of his native Italy. He knew only that it was no longer Catholic, and that was sufficient for him. God was singling him out to lead the way, by his prayers, to that country's conversion; God was calling him to be an Apostle to the English. The history of Paul of the Cross' devotion to the cause of England's reconversion is not long, although, it lasted for over a half century of his life. In old age, he was to relate to his fellow Passionists: "It is now fifty years since I began to pray unceasingly for the conversion of England to the faith of its fathers." So who was this Paul who developed such a passion for the English people?

Paul was born on 3 January 1694 in Ovada in the republic of Genoa; at this time Italy was a collection of independent states, each with their own laws and taxes. The Danei family was devout and included an uncle who was a priest. Paul's father, Luca, opened a shop selling cloth in Ovada, and it was here that he met his first wife who died after five years of marriage leaving him childless. He remarried and went on to have fifteen children, but only six survived to adulthood, and all lived to a ripe old age. A year after Paul's birth, his brother John Baptist was born, and the two would remain close throughout their lives.

Despite her many pregnancies and in poor health, their mother never failed to share her faith with them. Paul recalls that if he cried while she was combing his hair, she would show him a crucifix and say: "see how much Jesus has suffered." She would tell them about the lives of the saints, and in particular about the hermits in the desert, and it was these stories that gave Paul a great desire to serve God. When her children vexed her, she would sigh: "May God make saints of you all!" The brothers were taught to read and write, but not all went smoothly in the Danei family. Luca was not a businessman, and his story has various references to him being involved in fraud and smuggling tobacco (apparently involving Paul and John Baptist, and on one occasion Paul was shot by bandits and had to hand over all the smuggled tobacco); Luca's defence was that different laws applied in different regions! Inevitably when Luca got into legal difficulties it often resulted in the family having to move yet again. It is worth noting here that all his life Paul took snuff, and decreed that his religious were to be supplied with snuff!

Paul had been taught to read and write, eventually moving to Genoa to pursue his studies, and while there met a woman who was a mystic and she became his spiritual director. At the age of 19 Paul heard a sermon which brought about his "conversion to a life of penance." However, he immediately began to doubt the authenticity of what had happened. The question for him was: "Is God there? Or am I deceiving myself?" Eventually he went to church to seek consolation, and on Pentecost Sunday he had an intense experience in prayer and his doubts left him.

Prayer meant much to Paul, especially from the time he heard a moving sermon on the sufferings of Jesus. The Passion of Jesus gave new direction and meaning to Paul. He wanted to know Christ and the power of his love. He also wanted to share this Good News Gospel with others. He realised that many of his contemporaries did not know the true meaning of life. In the 18th century life was not easy. The rich were very rich and the poor were very poor. For the sick there was little healing; for labourers few hours of rest; for ordinary people there was the constant fear of war and bloodshed. Paul found an answer to this suffering in the story of Jesus' Passion. But how could he share his understanding with his neighbours?

In 1715 Pope Clement XI called for a crusade against the Ottoman empire. Paul saw this as his chance to do something for God, if necessary giving his life, and so he joined the army. After several months with the army going nowhere for a variety of political reasons, he attended the Forty Hours Devotion (a devotion of prayer in front of the Blessed Sacrament for forty hours) and was inspired to leave the army; whether he did this legally, or in fact deserted, is not clear, but he spent the next couple of years wandering around the country volunteering help where it was needed.

During this time two tensions emerged in Paul's life: he felt a tremendous attraction to live a life of solitude, to be a hermit, but at the same time his priest-uncle invited him to come and live with him, which he did in 1718. This allowed Paul to live a life of prayer, but his uncle had other plans for him and started to make arrangements for him to be married. Paul explained he had taken a private vow of chastity[1] and so could not marry, but the uncle was not to be thwarted and wrote to Rome for Paul to be dispensed from his vow; Paul simply had to trust in God. The matter was resolved when negotiations about the dowry collapsed, and shortly afterwards his uncle died. Paul was the sole beneficiary of a substantial estate,

---

[1] *A personal vow rather than one taken in public and recognised by the Church.*

but renounced everything in favour of his brothers and sisters, apart from his uncle's breviary[2].

Paul moved to Castellazzo in Piedmont where he recorded that every day he "spent at least seven hours in prayer and other religious activities," this included at least five hours in front of the Blessed Sacrament. At this time in Italy there were many confraternities for both men and women, and the members would read from books on prayer or discuss the Scriptures. Paul joined the Confraternity of St. Anthony of the Desert and was soon elected prior or leader and his talks inspired others. One major book to influence his own thought and teaching was the *Treatise on the Love of God* by St. Francis de Sales.

Paul thought in terms of priesthood, but in the Italy of his day, there were so many priests that one more would make little difference. He thought of joining one of the religious communities in his hometown, but the monks seemed to live in walled-in monasteries, unable to effectively minister to the people. He thought of going away to live a solitary life of meditation, but then who would go out to the poor, the sick, the neglected in the villages and countryside?

---

[2] *A prayer book containing the various parts ofthe Prayer of the Church used by priests and monks each day.*

The inclination to live a penitential life would cause Paul to both abstain from food and even give away what little he had; his mother feared that he would give away all his clothes one day. However, this life of penance was steeped in a life of prayer. Frequently he would get up very early in the morning with his brother John Baptist to pray. On one occasion their father caught them scourging themselves by way of penance – a common penitential practice in those days, and he feared for their lives.

Slowly Paul began to discern the way God was calling him. He wrote: "I had the idea of wearing a poor black tunic of coarse cloth called arbagio, the ordinary wool fabric found in these parts; of going bare-foot, of living in very deep poverty – in short, by God's grace, leading a penitential life. This never again left my heart. I had an even greater inclination not simply to retire to the little chapel... ; it would be enough for me to withdraw into solitude either there or anywhere else. This I would do in response to God's loving invitation, for in his infinite goodness he was calling me to leave the world."

The prayer life of Paul was filled with many visions, some of them not from God, and it was only through experience that he learned to recognise their origin and validity. He also was racked by scruples, wondering again and again what was God's will.

Paul did not always enjoy good health, and about this time he suffered from a severe fever which led to him shouting blasphemies against God and Mary. His sister reports that she heard him, as he recovered, talking to two Capuchin priests, and she concluded from their conversations that he must have had a vision of hell.

"Tall, dark and handsome" would be a good description of Paul at this time, with the result that a number of young ladies in Castellazzo showed interest in him as a potential husband. To try and fend them off he stopped shaving and cutting his fingernails, and also failed to change his clothes. Despite this behaviour he enjoyed a large circle of friends who clearly enjoyed his company. Interestingly a number of these young men went on to become priests or Religious[3].

The spiritual life of Paul was shaped increasingly by inspirations he received in prayer; in particular, he recognised that he was being called to gather companions to form a community, and the hallmark of the community would be a life of penance. Crucially Paul saw all of this in a positive light and recognised that God wanted him to share his love with people. From here on Paul accepted that whenever he had a special grace or consolation in prayer,

---

[3] *A member of a Religious Order, either a Priest or lay Brother.*

it was normally by way of preparing him for a severe trial. Recognising that he could easily be misled in his prayer he searched for a spiritual director – a search which was not always successful; the parish priest at the time was particularly unhelpful and eventually admitted he was out of his depth and so referred him on to the Capuchins.

During 1717 the idea constantly came into Paul's mind during prayer that one day he would wear a black habit, but whether as a hermit or a monk in an existing Order was not made clear. One day as he struggled with this question Our Lady appeared to him dressed in a black tunic with a badge of the Passion over her breast. She said to him: "Have you noticed son, that I am wearing a dress of mourning? That is for the painful Passion of my beloved son, Jesus. You too must dress like this and found a Congregation in which the same dress will be worn, and in which there will be continuing mourning over the Passion and death of my dear Son." Paul doubted the validity of the vision and was reluctant to act on it, and yet he had no doubt that Our Lady had spoken. Seeking clarity and consolation in prayer, all he received was warnings of trials ahead: "He who comes close to me comes close to thorns!" After consulting various people Paul did not know what to do and waited in an agony of uncertainty and sheer terror.

Writing in 1720 Paul says: "This last summer (I do not remember the day or the month because I did not write it down, but I do know it was the grain harvest time) on a certain weekday in the Capuchin church in Castellazzo, I received holy Communion with a deep sense of my unworthiness. I remember that I was deeply recollected, and then I left to go home. Walking along the street I was as recollected as if I were at prayer. When I came to a street corner to turn towards home, I was raised up in God in the deepest recollection, with complete forgetfulness of all else and with great interior peace. At that moment I saw myself clothed in a long black garment with a white cross on my breast, and below the cross the holy name of Jesus was written in white letters. At that instant I heard these very words spoken to me: 'This signifies how pure and spotless that heart should be which must bear the holy name of Jesus graven upon it.' On seeing and hearing this I began to weep and then it stopped. Shortly afterwards I saw in spirit the tunic presented to me with the holy name of Jesus and the cross all in white, but the tunic was black. I pressed it joyfully to my heart."

Paul also recorded: "After these visions of the tunic and the sign, God gave me a stronger compelling desire to gather companions and with the approval of Holy Mother Church to found a Congregation called 'The Poor of Jesus'. After this God infused in my soul in a lasting manner the form of the holy Rule[4] to be observed by the Poor of Jesus and by me his least and lowest servant… Let it be known that the intention God gave me with regard to this Congregation was none other than this: in the first place to observe God's law perfectly together with the perfect observance of his evangelical counsels[5], especially by total detachment from all created things with the perfect practice of holy poverty, so essential for the observance of the other counsels and for maintaining fervour at prayer; in the second place to have zeal for God's glory, to promote the fear of God in souls by working for the destruction of sin, in a word, to be indefatigable in works of charity that our beloved God may be loved, feared, served and praised by all for ever and ever. Amen."

Paul was a man of his times, and a man of the Church, and went to see his Bishop for guidance. He asked to be allowed to serve in the Church as a solitary, a hermit. At the same time Paul was experiencing the call to form a religious community. The founding of a Religious Congregation would not be an easy task, and Paul realised that first he would need the support of the local

---

[4] *A Rule is a way of life set out in a document to guide the members of a Religious Order to live a way of life approved by the Church and similar to the original inspiration of the founder of the Order.*

Bishop, Francesco Gattinara. Despite various obstacles being put in his way, a meeting with the Bishop finally took place. Paul began by making his confession to the Bishop and then described the inspirations he had about wearing the black habit and living in poverty. The Bishop was moved to tears and asked Paul to write a full account, and it is because of this that we know so much about what actually happened. The Bishop felt that he was not competent to help Paul and so referred him to two wise and holy Jesuits. Paul was clothed in the black habit (as inspired in the vision of Our Lady) by Bishop Gattinara on 22 November 1720, and then began to live a fully penitential life.

All looked as if Paul would now be able to confidently set out to live his vocation, but as the date for his clothing in the habit approached he experienced a series of doubts and depressions and again questioned whether he was being deceived. At the same time, he lost all sense of devotion and consolation in prayer, and so to actually spend time in prayer became almost a physical struggle. He had severe doubts that he would not be

---

[5] *The three evangelical counsels, or counsels of perfection, are chastity, poverty, and obedience, as Jesus of Nazareth stated in the gospels; they are counsels for those who desire to become "perfect". The difference between a precept and a counsel is, that the precept is a matter of necessity while the counsel is left to the free choice of the person.*

able to persevere in his vocation and felt that the devil was suggesting there were other less demanding ways to respond to God.

Having been clothed in the black habit, Paul was now officially a hermit; this was not an unusual way of life in Italy, as men would live alone, care for a chapel, and maybe teach catechism and help people to pray. The Bishop was happy for Paul to give catechism and teach people to pray, but he had doubts about his founding a Congregation. Following his clothing Paul left the Bishop and returned to the church of San Carlo in Castellazzo and moved into the little room behind the sacristy where he was to live for the next forty days. Bishop Gattinara had instructed Paul to keep a diary of what happened during the retreat[6] and also write the Rule of life for the Poor of Jesus. Paul had been chosen by God for a very specific mission, and yet he was to see the most unexpected obstacles rise in his path – hardly surprising for someone who was called to follow his master to Calvary.

---

[6] *A period of leaving one's normal life and spending time, often in solitude and prayer, for a set period of time, maybe up to forty days long. Later, the monasteries Paul established were all called Retreats, especially as they were in isolated places.*

CHAPTER 2

THE HERMIT

Paul moved into what was effectively the hermitage at Castellazzo on 23 November 1720 and remained there until 1 January 1721, living solely on bread and water, sleeping a few hours each night, wrapped in a blanket, and stretched out on vine branches formed to make a bed. From the first day he began to record his inspirations and temptations, the desolations and consolations. The forty days not only imitated the time of Jesus in the desert, it also led Paul into a battleground where he would struggle to pray, resist evil, and respond to God's grace. Underpinning all of this was the full awareness of the reality of God's love as shown in the Passion of Jesus.

The Spiritual Diary which Paul wrote at this time is seen by experts as a classic of mystical prayer. It presents Paul talking with Jesus about the various tortures experienced during the Passion, and it evokes in Paul a deep awareness of his own sins. He makes it clear that this is not an intellectual process, but something that takes place deep within the heart; it is the realisation that despite our failure to love God, God's love is total and unconditional, God never stops loving us – the only adequate response is to love as well as we can in return.

The hermitage proved not to be a place of quiet solitude, nor a place for leisurely prayer, but a spiritual battleground, in addition to the severe physical privations he underwent. Paul knew he had to write the Rule for the Poor of Jesus, but it is necessary to point out that he had no training in Church Law, and had no formal theological training, in fact he had never read a Religious Rule. Aware of this he entrusted himself to the guidance of the Holy Spirit. He wrote:

"I began to write the Rule in the year 1720 on 2nd. December and finished on the 7th. of the same month. Before writing I said Matins[7] before daybreak and spent some time in mental prayer. Then I left prayer full of courage and began to write. The infernal enemy did not fail to assault me by stirring up feelings of repugnance within me, and making difficulties about my doing this. But since God had inspired me to this task, and as I had been given orders to do it, without more ado by God's grace I set to work."

---

[7] *Part of the monastic prayer of the Church, often said in the middle of the night.*

He continued: "Let it be known that when I was writing, I wrote as quickly as if someone were dictating to me; I felt the words coming from the heart. I have written this to make it known that this was a special inspiration from God because as for myself I am but wickedness and ignorance. In all, however, I submit to the judgement of my superiors. May the Blessed Sacrament on all the altars of the whole world be praised and adored by all."

After Paul received Communion it was not unusual for him to receive further inspirations and consolations. He gradually formed the idea that a primary work of the Poor of Jesus would be to reach out to those who were not experiencing the love of God, the fruit of the Passion of Jesus. On the day he finished writing the Rule Paul noted: "I had likewise great fervour mingled with tears in praying for the conversion of poor sinners; I kept telling God that I could no longer bear to see him offended. I had also special tenderness in imploring God in his mercy to found the holy Congregation quickly, and to send forth some people for his greater glory and for the good of their neighbours – this with great desire and fervour. I asked him to accept me as the least and lowest servant of his poor, and it seemed to me that I was utterly unworthy (as indeed I am) to serve him."

Central to his life of prayer was the contemplation of the Passion, not simply as a pious remembering of the Calvary-event, but something that was alive and active today.

In the Spiritual Diary, the entry records for Thursday, December 26, 1720, the feast of St. Stephen the first martyr: "I had the special desire for the conversion of heretics, and especially of England with its neighbouring kingdoms, and I made special prayer for this during Most Holy Communion." This was linked with a desire "to die a martyr's death in a place where the adorable mystery of the Eucharist is denied." Again, three days later, Paul writes: "... and I had a particular impulse to pray for the conversion of England; especially because I want the standard of the holy Faith to be erected, so that there will be an increase of devotion and reverence, of homage and love, with frequent acts of adoration for the Blessed Sacrament, the ineffable mystery of God's most holy love, and so that His Holy Name may be glorified in a very special way. The desire to die as a martyr, especially for the Blessed Sacrament, in some place where people do not believe, does not leave me." Paul emerged from the forty-day retreat with a mysterious zeal for the conversion of England, a zeal which endured until his death.

It is possible that Paul's knowledge of England stemmed from his awareness of the life and death of St. Thomas of Canterbury. It is also reasonable to assume that as Castellazzo was on the pilgrim route from England to Rome, he heard not only about persecution and martyrdoms brought about by the Reformation, but also the state of the Church in England from travelling pilgrims.

From this time to the end of his life, Paul was to pray "unceasingly" – his own term – for England. Blessed Vincent Strambi's "Life of St. Paul of the Cross:" says: "England was always the country of his preference. It might almost seem to some who knew him well, as if he had no heart, no feeling but for England. England was always in his thoughts; England was constantly the subject of his discourses; England was always before him in his prayers."

Carrying the Rule and his Spiritual Diary Paul set out to see Bishop Gattinara with the hope of obtaining approval of the Rule. Several young men, including his brother John Baptist had declared their intention of joining Paul in the new community. However, the Bishop advised him not to go to Rome to seek approval, but instead to go to Fr. Columban, a Capuchin, and seek his opinion of the Rule. Paul set off in the middle of winter on the 60 kilometre journey, and was nearly killed by the snow and the cold, only surviving due to the charity of some policemen; Paul was eternally grateful to those policemen.

Having consulted Fr. Columban, the Capuchin told Paul he felt that the Rule could be submitted to Rome. He returned to meet with the Bishop, but he was still reluctant to give his approval. He asked Paul to move to another hermitage two miles from Castellazzo, but he did allow him to form groups for catechesis. Paul remained there only a couple of weeks because he felt, despite its solitude, it was too far from the Blessed Sacrament and therefore unsuitable. Having obtained the Bishop's consent, he moved to the hermitage of San Stefano close to the Capuchin church.

As a catechist Paul was highly successful, and when the Bishop heard glowing reports about him, he authorised him to preach from the pulpit in the church every Sunday. These sermons were very popular and attracted a steady following. From this a group of young men emerged who shared not only their prayer, but also their meals with Paul; but the fact remains that most of the food was given away to the poor.

Sometimes Paul's sermons would last two hours, but everyone seemed happy with them, and many accounts emerged of people changing their way of life. His sermons would deal with the Sacrament of Reconciliation, love for the Eucharist, knowledge of the Faith, and how to meditate on the Passion. In addition to giving spiritual direction to the laity Paul also directed a number of priests and nuns.

The urge to go to Rome was still very strong and so he asked the Bishop for his permission. However, Bishop Gattinara was reluctant to agree, mainly because he was not keen on Paul gathering companions as he felt there were too many Religious Orders. Eventually, in April 1720 the Bishop wrote a letter of recommendation for Paul, but there seemed little point in going to Rome then as Clement XI had died. The following month, in record time, Innocent XIII had been elected Pope, so in August Paul set off for Rome. He planned to sail from Genoa, and John Baptist asked to go with him. Paul refused to take him, and John Baptist warned him "Go alone if you wish, but you will have no peace without me."

The journey was uneventful until the ship was becalmed off the coast of Monte Argentario, a mountain set in the sea, but not quite an island. When Paul discovered the name of the mountain his heart gave a jump, for this was a place to which he had often been invited in prayer by Our Lady.

For centuries hermits had lived there – a place of isolation and beauty; Paul felt a strong attraction to live there for the rest of his life. Arriving in Rome he went to pray in St. Peter's but only experienced desolation in his prayer. He moved on to the Pilgrim's hospice where he stayed for two nights, and was amazed to have his feet washed by a Jesuit Cardinal; he gratefully accepted the gift of two loaves of bread. Paul must have looked like a real beggar, as he tried to see the Pope, with the result that he was thrown out from the Papal Palace into the street – to see the Pope was not as easy as seeing his Bishop!

His dream was shattered, he could not see a way forward and so went to sit by a fountain to eat his one remaining loaf. At which point a poor man came and begged for bread: Paul shared half his loaf. He then walked into the Basilica of St. Mary Major with the intention of entrusting his mission to Mary. The icon of Mary is said to have been painted by St. Luke, and kneeling in front of it Paul prayed for understanding. Slowly he realised that it was not yet the time for presenting the Rule to the Pope. In the meantime, he must be faithful to the inspiration God had given him. Before the icon of Mary, he made a vow to promote the memory of the Passion of Jesus and to work to gather companions for this purpose.

CHAPTER 3

MONTE ARGENTARIO

Paul realised he had to return home, but first he wanted to take a closer look at Monte Argentario. As he was penniless, he set off from Rome on foot, and for accommodation relied on the hospitality of Religious Communities. He recognised that as he had apparently failed in his mission, Bishop Gattinara would not give him permission to gather companions. Inevitably Paul's thoughts turned back to being a solitary hermit; he had been told about an old hermitage on Monte Argentario dedicated to Our Lady of the Annunciation, and decided to inspect it before going to see Bishop Salvi, the local Bishop.

Having seen the hermitage, Paul had to walk about seventy miles in the heat before meeting Bishop Salvi who gave him permission to live at the hermitage. Paul headed back to Genoa another arduous journey, and had a meeting with Bishop Gattinara who listened to Paul's account of his visit to Rome, and agreed to clothe John Baptist in the black habit exactly one year after he had clothed Paul. The brothers remained in Castellazzo for the winter, during which time Paul wrote to Bishop Salvi asking permission to bring companions to Monte Argentario; the Bishop refused, saying he could bring only one companion. The Bishop was not being obstructive, but while he could give permission to hermits, it required papal approval to form a community.

In April 1722 the two brothers arrived at the hermitage of the Annunciation which proved to be a large but sparse and primitive building. They spent their days in prayer and study, rising at midnight for three hours of prayer and meditation. Much of their time was spent in silence, the better to listen to God. For food they relied solely on charity, but since they spent so much time fasting, their requirements were minimal. On Sundays they taught catechism in the two neighbouring villages; and this way of life continued for a full year.

Having heard about the sanctity of the two brothers, the Bishop of Gaeta invited them to come and work in his diocese, catechising and taking care of the sick and dying. They agreed and moved to a new hermitage. The Bishop was so impressed by Paul that he asked him to preach in the cathedral, and also to conduct the spiritual exercises for the students preparing for ordination – this generated a certain amount of jealousy among the local clergy given that Paul was a layman.

In 1724 they were invited by Bishop Cavalieri of Troia, who was the uncle of St. Alphonsus Ligouri, to work in his diocese. He was particularly interested in their desire to practice continuous adoration in front of the Blessed Sacrament, and had expressed the intention of joining the Institute one day. They were not able to fulfil this intention of adoration in front of the Blessed Sacrament because they were so heavily involved in preaching and catechesis. The brothers agreed to move to the diocese of Troia, but were forced to spend six months living in the Bishop's Palace! Whilst there the Bishop offered to revise the text of the Rule, and also suggested it would be easier to have the Rule approved if they were ordained, given that laymen could never rule over a clerical institute.

Benedict XIII was now on the papal throne: a Dominican who rejected the pomp of the Vatican, and who had even built himself a hermitage. He was a radical reformer, firmly rooted in Gospel values. He declared 1725 to be a Holy Year, and convoked a Roman Council. Bishop Cavalieri was prevented from attending by poor health, so Paul and John Baptist were delighted to go in his place, carrying several letters of introduction, in the hope that this would enable them to gain papal approval for the Rule.

On arriving in Rome they met Monsignor Crescenzi, who at 30 was a year younger than Paul. He became a faithful friend and benefactor, and was instrumental in arranging for the brothers to meet the Pope in May 1725. At that meeting Benedict XIII gave verbal permission to the brothers to gather together companions – unfortunately they did not get this permission in writing.

In the light of this development Paul and John Baptist returned to Gaeta. Bishop Cavalieri had wanted them to return to Troia, and wanted them to found a new Congregation under his control; this is certainly not what Paul had envisaged. In Gaeta Paul experienced challenges on political, ecclesiastical, and social fronts. This resulted in his moving from Gaeta to Itri, but even in Itri the hermitage was tied up by rules of patronage, and so Paul had to accept that long term development there would be impossible.

Problems began to develop: things had not worked out at Gaeta, and there was no possibility of development in Troia as Bishop Cavalieri had died. There was still Monte Argentario, but they could live there only as hermits – they could not gather companions to establish a community. Paul decided the brothers should return to Rome and move into the new hospital in Trastevere. They believed that here they could offer themselves totally to God, and would remain there permanently. In October 1726 Benedict XIII consecrated the church of the hospital of San Gallicano, and the brothers were entrusted with the spiritual care of the patients. Catechism groups were quickly established, and patients were soon being prepared for Holy Communion.

In March 1727 Paul wrote to a friend: "The superiors wish us to be ordained priests, continuing, with the Pope's permission, in the same habit and life-style as at present." If ordination was to take place, then clearly the brothers would have to undertake some formal theological studies. This they did at a Franciscan college close to Trastevere. At the end of their studies they made a retreat under the direction of the Jesuits at the Quirinal palace, and were ordained sub-deacons in the Basilica of St. John Lateran. On 7 June they were ordained to the priesthood by Benedict XIII in St. Peter's.

Towards the end of July 1727 Luca Danei, their father, died. It took two months for the brothers to return to Castellazzo, and when they did arrive they were both suffering from malaria – because of this it was eighteen days before Paul could celebrate Mass. While in Castellazzo the brothers renounced their share of their father's inheritance. Soon they returned to San Gallicano where they discovered plans had been developed to change the way the hospital was run, changes which would make it difficult for Paul and John Baptist to remain there.

By way of explanation Paul wrote: "We discovered that new Constitutions were being drawn up for the hospital, and one of the principal treatments for those suffering from ringworm was blood-letting from the head. Although this is a work of great charity we hadn't the heart to do it, and in fact we were never required to do it. We were fully occupied in all other duties of charity, especially in the spiritual care of the sick etc., but never in this. We have seen His Eminence the Cardinal Protector[8], who to ensure proper discipline in the place, and greater uniformity in the community, required everyone to take part in the above-mentioned duty and in other works of charity (which I omit for brevity's sake). Since we had no heart for it (according to our way of doing it), His Eminence has very kindly procured a Brief for us from His Holiness to allow us to retire into solitude and to persevere in our own life-style etc. And so it has turned out by God's grace."

In other words, Paul could see that the new Constitutions were incorporating the brothers into an institution which they were not in fact called to. But because of their initial vow of perseverance[9] on joining the hospital it was necessary for them to be dispensed from this vow

---

[8] *A Cardinal who would look after a particular Order or charitable work, and act as their "friend at court."*

by the Holy Father. The request was made in February 1728, just eighteen months after they had arrived at the hospital.

The dispensation from the vow did not leave the brothers free to do or go where they wanted. Every priest had to have what is called a title of ordination stating where he ministered and who his Superior was. In its simplest form a diocesan priest is under the jurisdiction of his Bishop, and a Religious priest is under his Superior. But in the case of Paul and John Baptist they were neither Diocesan nor Religious Priests. Paul and John Baptist had been ordained to work in the hospital, but once they left there, they would be seen as drifters. When the Pope gave them a dispensation, he gave them permission to say Mass for a year, during which they would have to find a new title under which to exercise their ministry. The reality of the San Gallicano experience is that while they were doing good and charitable work, it is not what God was asking of them. Ultimately they felt called to live a life of solitude, and that meant living in a solitary place and live according to their own Rule. Yet again they felt the call to return to the hermitage on Monte Argentario.

---

[9] *Every priest has to work under the jurisdiction of a Bishop or Religious Superior to prevent priests from drifting around the country. In this case Paul and John Baptist, by vow, were attached to the specific hospital of San Gallicano.*

CHAPTER 4

LAYING DOWN ROOTS

In March 1728 the brothers returned to the hermitage of the Annunciation on Monte Argentario, only to discover that somebody else had moved in and was planning to establish a community there, living according to a Rule he himself had written. Paul and John Baptist asked to join him, but he became angry and chased them away.

Deciding to return to Castellazzo they went down the mountain and got into a boat, but the boat became becalmed, so they knelt in the boat and prayed for guidance. Possibly God did not want them to leave, so they returned to shore, disembarked, and the wind sprang up again. Back on Monte Argentario they discovered another hermitage, Sant' Antonio, on the other side of the mountain. Having obtained the local priest's permission, they moved in to what was an almost derelict building, which of course suited them perfectly! The new Bishop allowed the brothers to remain there, and also accept others who wished to join the community.

A number of young men joined the brothers, but none were able to cope with the rigorous life and returned home. In May 1730 their brother Antonio, arrived to see them; he was so impressed by their way of life that he decided to remain. He made a retreat, was clothed in the black habit, was ordained and became an excellent missioner. After several years he left, apparently unable to cope with the solitude. However, a year after leaving he returned and remained another twenty years, before finally returning to Castellazzo where he lived a long and devout priestly life.

One difficulty at Sant' Antonio was that there was only a small chapel and two rooms, one above the other. This forced Paul to think about building a house for both a larger community and also for people who may want to come on retreat – a word which was eventually adopted for all Passionist monasteries or communities. One description of Sant' Antonio describes the upstairs room as the bedroom: beds were made from sacks filled with straw and set on boards. Rising at midnight they spent three hours in prayer, then rest before rising for more prayer and Mass. Time for study followed, before community celebration of the Divine Office, followed by a frugal lunch, the fruit of charitable donations. A period of relaxation followed, then vespers and more study. Night prayer of the Church and mental prayer brought the day to the end.

Pastoral work for Paul and John Baptist was teaching catechism and hearing Confessions in the three nearest towns. But in 1730 they were asked to preach a series of missions[10]; this was a major development, especially as missions were so popular in the 18th century and provided an opportunity for catechesis and spiritual renewal. This was especially true in remote areas, and particularly in the mosquito infested marshlands of Tuscany, where a number of priests were unwilling to work.

Paul and John Baptist would leave Sant' Antonio, moving from mission to mission before returning to the solitude of the hermitage. In addition to the work of preaching and reconciliation, Paul also encountered many young men interested in pursuing a Religious vocation with Paul. Requests came in from more and more Bishops for missions to be preached, and at the same time lay people increasingly offered their support.

On Paul's first mission his preaching had a huge impact on a 27-year-old woman called Agnes Grazi. For the next

---

[10] *A period, often a fortnight, set aside in a parish for the preaching of sermons and instructions. The mission was designed to revitalise the life of individuals and the parish, and so often entailed encouraging people to return to the Sacraments, especially after using the Sacrament of Reconciliation or Confession.*

fourteen years she had Paul as her spiritual director, and he guided her to the heights of mystical prayer. Agnes died in 1744 but left well over 150 letters of direction from Paul.

In prayer Paul was inspired to build his first Retreat on the side of Monte Argentario. Of course he would need support from the people in the local town of Orbetello, including the family of Agnes Grazi. While the proposed site was on the land owned by the town, the revenue from it went to the Prior of Orbetello. An extraordinary complicated series of negotiations took place involving Paul, the council of Orbetello, the local Bishop, the Holy See, etc., etc. Trying to explain the situation Paul wrote to the Bishop of Alessandria:

"God's mercy is arranging for a Retreat [monastery] of Penance to be built for us and our companions upon a property held by the city of Orbetello. It consists of a church dedicated to the Presentation of the Blessed Virgin Mary (a day of special blessing for us as the day we entered upon our present way of life) with about eighteen small, poor rooms, etc. Besides this a retreat house will be built, not only for priests of the neighbouring dioceses (for in the bad climate of this marshy locality, hardly any have a seminary), but also for laymen who at convenient times would like to come here for spiritual exercises. A large quantity of material is already on the spot, and the foundation-stone will be laid very shortly. I am telling you all this as to our own pastor, to recommend this holy work to your prayers and also to those of your beloved flock. This Retreat is being built here on Monte Argentario close to where we are... When the Retreat is built, I hope that God's mercy will give us the grace to depend upon poverty, especially when others come. Already there are some who wish to do so, but we cannot receive them because we have no room."

Repeatedly Paul offered to supply more and more information to the ecclesiastical authorities, and he offered the names of possible referees, including Bishop Gattinara, now the Archbishop of Turin. Glowing references were obtained, including one from Bishop Palmieri who stated that the community could not be imitated without a special grace from God. He continued:

"They are priests who follow their own Rule, wearing a very rough black habit next to their bare skin...; they always go barefoot, with head uncovered. Living from what is spontaneously given to them, they observe a continual Lenten fast in the hermitage, and the little rest they have is taken on straw. They celebrate the Office in their little church, both during the day and in the middle of the night, and the remainder of their day they spend in mental prayer and in study.

"The senior of the group, Paul, ministers as a missionary with zeal and fervour, going from one diocese to another giving missions; this year he has given missions in my diocese and is now about to go to Piombino and other places in the diocese of Massa, in this Province of Siena. His younger brother, John Baptist, goes with him and gives catechesis, preaches spiritual exercises to the clergy and hears confessions. Both of them do a great deal for the spiritual growth of the people, both by their good example and by the word of God."

Paul was asked to preach a mission in Orbetello in 1733; he took the opportunity to remind the citizens that they had agreed to support the building of the new Retreat, but it looked as if they had withdrawn their support. He announced that because of this he and his community had decided to leave Monte Argentario and go elsewhere. This had the desired effect, and the citizens told Paul to leave everything in their hands. Paul returned to Monte Argentario and building work began immediately.

The building of the Retreat, and the preaching of missions and retreats, took place against a backdrop of the threat of wars involving Naples, Spain, the Garrison State, and Austria. Political, military and civil unrest underpinned every area Paul worked in. The Garrison State, to the north of Rome, was controlled by Austria, but Spain attacked it and won control of most of it; all that remained was to attack the capital of the Garrison State, Orbetello.

Because of earlier contacts with the General leading the Spanish forces, Paul was trusted by both sides, and so was given permission to pass from one camp to another, taking care of the wounded and dying. Because of its location Orbetello would not be taken easily; to facilitate its capture the Spanish General planned to shell the town from Monte Argentario. Paul pleaded with the General on behalf of the people of Orbetello, and eventually the General gave way and agreed not to launch a bombing campaign.

Finally, the Austrian garrison surrendered, but Paul and John Baptist had already set off to give some missions in the Isle of Elba. On this journey they met two men who would eventually join the community, one of whom, Tommaso Fossi joined at the age of fifty-six after the death of his wife, having fathered eight children. While the two older brothers were away, younger brother Antonio supervised the building of the new Retreat, supported by the people of Orbetello. However, the war had caused money to dry up, and so it was suggested that Paul should go and visit King Charles III of Naples who had already approved the founding of the Retreat of the Presentation. Paul and John Baptist met the King in January 1736 and were warmly welcomed; the King gave the brothers a substantial donation to help with the building work, so that by October the roof and walls were finished.

Despite his mystical experience in prayer, or maybe because of it, Paul was very practical. He wrote to Tommaso Fossi:

"Were it not for lack of funds we would enter it on the feast of the Presentation, but we are short of timbers to make the doors and window-frames. If you could find a little for us there and also procure some in Marciana, it would be a great act of charity. It would then be our business to have it brought here provided we can find someone to manage a load of wood for us... Others wish to come [to join the community] but the retreat is not finished. What a help it would be to have a few planks of seasoned timber."

By the summer of 1737 the building work was finished. Paul wrote to the Cardinal for permission to have the church blessed as a public oratory[11], but as in previous negotiations the Cardinal was not co-operative, and wanted the church to be a private oratory for sole use of the community. At the heart of the issue was the fact that the Cardinal still had not transferred ownership of some of the land; part of the reason for his opposition was that he wanted to alter the Rule, in particular the refusal to have any fixed sources of income. The Cardinal cited the example of the Jesuits who, he claimed, had started out that way, but had learned it was not practical. Fortunately, the Cardinal's Vicar General, supporting Paul, stated that this kind of absolute poverty was the principal distinguishing characteristic of the new Congregation.

Without the Cardinal's permission to have the church blessed, the nine members of the community would have to walk from the new Retreat to Sant' Antonio, more than a mile, to celebrate Mass. Writing to the Cardinal, Paul described the situation:

---

[11] *An oratory is a structure other than a parish church, set aside by ecclesiastical authority for prayer and the celebration of Mass. It is for all intents and purposes another word for what is commonly called a chapel, except a few oratories are set up for the Divine Office and prayers but not Mass. Previously, canon law distinguished several types of oratories: private (with use restricted to an individual, such as a bishop, or group, such as a family, or public (built for the benefit of any of the faithful who wish to use it).*

"At present we are living in a poor hovel, so small and wretched that anyone who sees so many living in it is moved to compassion. The simple fact is that the four lay brothers sleep in a single hut; because the place is so small and the hot weather coming on, we are infested with a huge number of fleas and other filth, and there is no way of dealing with them."

This had no influence on the Cardinal, despite Paul writing at least another seven letters, but to no avail. Clearly there was opposition to the church of the Presentation being made a public oratory; certainly some priests and Religious opposed the opening of the new church, fearing people would go there instead of to the churches in Orbetello.

Finally, the Cardinal agreed to transfer ownership of the land, but he still opposed the opening of the church. Paul was forced, by Cardinal Altieri, to write to Rome for permission to have the church blessed as a private oratory. But before the letter reached Rome two of Paul's friends had obtained a letter from Pope Clement XII giving permission for the church to be blessed as a public oratory, thus obtaining for Paul what he wanted from the beginning. Nevertheless, it was another four years before Cardinal Altieri would give permission to reserve the Blessed Sacrament.

On 14 September, the feast of the Exaltation of the Cross, the solemn blessing of the church took place. The community of five priests and four lay brothers finally had a home.

CHAPTER 5

SEEKING APPROVAL

Now that the Retreat of the Presentation had been built, much of 1737 was spent by Paul giving missions and retreats. The name "The Poor of Jesus" was changed to "The discalced clerics of the Holy Cross and Passion of Jesus Christ". Paul stipulated that half of the community must remain at home in the community praying while the other half is out giving missions. A balance also had to be maintained between the active apostolic life and the contemplative life of prayer for each individual. He was never one to worry about numbers, but for Paul what was important was that the community should be made up of men of deep prayer, content to spend long periods meditating on the Passion; if they could not do this Paul did not believe they could teach others to pray. He said that while preaching missions the priests should teach the people how to pray by meditating aloud.

The Rule still had not been approved so Paul went to Rome early in 1738. He did receive permission to preach anywhere in Italy, but he was not able to get approval of the Rule. Some claimed that the Rule was so severe that the Pope refused to grant approval, but the Pope was very ill and was expected to die at any time. However, the fact remained that most of those who had entered the Retreat of the Presentation had now left.

By 1739 Paul had lost a number of his allies in Rome either due to illness or people moving from Rome. Cardinal Rezzonico of Venice had been recommended as a supporter of the little Congregation. It was not until February 1740 that the Pope finally died, and then the conclave to elect the new Pope dragged on for six months – the longest conclave of the eighteenth century. Finally, Benedict XIV was elected Pope.

Cardinal Rezzonico explained to the Pope the aims of the new Institute and won his approval; now all Paul had to do was bring the Constitutions to Rome for examination and hopefully approval. In November 1740 Paul and John Baptist presented the Rule to the Pope who, after reading it, commented "This Congregation of the Passion of Jesus Christ should have been the first to be founded, and it has arrived at last." A papal commission was established to examine the Rule and the brothers returned to Monte Argentario for Christmas. However, Paul was anxious the Commission would alter the Rule, and in particular add pastoral work other than Missions, thus changing the spirit of the Congregation. Consequently, he wrote to each member of the Commission:

"The most effective means of rooting out vice and planting true reverence is meditation on the most bitter pains of our Divine Saviour, and since the majority of the faithful live in forgetfulness of how much our most loveable Jesus has done and suffered, and because of this spend their lives sleeping soundly in the horrible quagmire of wickedness, zealous workers, poor in spirit and detached from all created things are needed to waken them from this detestable lethargy, so that with the trumpet of the word of God, and by means of the most holy Passion of Jesus Christ, they may waken those poor sinners who 'sit in darkness and in the shadow of death', so that God will be glorified in so many converted souls and in many others who will devote themselves to learning how to pray and, in this way, to holiness of life."

For thirty years Paul left his Retreat or monastery always on foot, for courses of missions which lasted two or three months at a time. On missions he rose early and made lengthy preparations for Mass. After Mass there was half an hour's meditation on the Passion, followed by an instruction on the Commandments which lasted an hour. Most of the rest of the day was spent hearing Confessions. The evening service lasted about an hour and a half and consisted of an instruction, sermon and meditation on the Passion. Then followed more Confessions. Any "spare" time was spent visiting the sick.

The Rule was approved in May 1741, thus allowing the Religious to make public rather than private vows[12]. They were also allowed to wear the Passionist "sign" – Paul had waited more than 20 years for his vision to be fulfilled, and now the climax was reached when permission was given to reserve the Blessed Sacrament in the chapel of the Retreat of the Presentation. Six companions, including Paul and John Baptist made a ten-day retreat before taking the traditional vows of Poverty, Chastity, Obedience, and adding a fourth distinctive vow to promote in the hearts of the people the memory of the Passion of Jesus.

Now that the Institute was formally established and had ecclesiastical approval, vocations started to come at a faster rate, including a number of men who had already been ordained priests. By 1743 the Retreat was full, leading Paul to consider establishing two new Retreats, but hopes and disappointments had become his way

---

[12] *A public vow is one which is recognized as such by the Church; otherwise it is private.*

of life. His missions were so influential that a people of a town where he had preached would offer him an isolated plot of land for a Retreat. The people of Vetralla did precisely that and said the town council would pay the costs; the site they offered already had a hermitage and a small chapel dedicated to St. Michael. Religious jealousies got in the way and the Capuchins objected, preventing any possible development – Paul decided to wait a year.

Vocations continued to come and Paul was advised to establish communities in the Papal States "so as to be more visible to the Court of Rome, in order that the Congregation might become better known, and may be even more esteemed on account of that austere, penitential life... to which the Lord has called you." At the end of December 1743 Pope Benedict XIV authorised the founding of communities in Vetralla and Toscanella.

Before the Retreat at Toscanella could be built, Paul was asked to establish a community at Sant' Eutizio in Soriano where there was a recently built church and monastery. In the normal course of events establishing such a community could take months and even years of negotiation between local, state, and ecclesiastical authorities. On this occasion Paul enjoyed the support of two brothers, both of whom were powerful and influential Cardinals and who had connections with Soriano. Paul accepted the offer but worried about not having enough men to establish both the community at Vetralla and another at Soriano. The problem was removed when Paul discovered that one of the Cardinals had "obtained permission from His Holiness not only to admit twelve religious to profession, with a dispensation from some months of the noviciate[13] to be given at my discretion, but also to have a number of religious ordained with the title of poverty."

In fact, Toscanella was nowhere near ready for anyone to move in, and of course Paul was not looking for anything elaborate, simply a roof and four walls, along with a suitable chapel – he was not concerned with furniture etc. In March 1744 Paul received the profession of vows of eight novices, one of whom, already a priest, would become the Superior in Soriano by the end of the week. Paul set off from Monte Argentario to Vetralla, a journey which took four days, accompanied by the new Superior Fr. Marcaurelio, two more priests, a few Brothers and six students. On their arrival they were welcomed by the clergy and civic leaders, and

[13] *The noviciate is normally a minimum of twelve months spent in isolation in one house, not only learning about the spirituality of the Congregation, but also discerning if one is suitable to live such a life. At the end of this time a person would make their vows.*

Paul reported that all the correct legal procedures were followed for handing over the property. John Baptist, who had supervised much of the work, was left as the Superior of the new Retreat.

From Vetralla Paul, Marcaurelio, two priests and the students went to Soriano. By 1744 the Congregation had grown rapidly: there were communities at Monte Argentario, Vetralla and Soriano, and now there were seventeen professed Religious. Paul was conscious that the approval for the Rule was only valid as long as Benedict XIV remained alive, he now wanted solemn approbation of the Congregation. The Pope established another commission to examine the Rule, but by January 1745 Paul had returned to Monte Argentario. On the journey he caught a chill which forced him to remain in bed for five months in the family home of Agnes Grazi.

Paul had travelled from Rome with Tommaso Struzzieri who wished to join the Congregation. Tommaso was 38 and had been a priest for fifteen years; he had received a doctorate in law, and had spent much of his time preaching missions. He arrived at Monte Argentario in January 1745, began his noviciate, and after three months made his profession of vows – the usual time for a noviciate is twelve months, but Paul had been given permission to make a number of dispensations.

The work of the commission dragged on through 1745, causing Paul considerable anxiety as he heard reports of some of the discussions. A few members of the commission wanted the student communities to have a stable source of income, rather than rely solely on charity and the providence of God. Paul was strongly opposed to this, believing it would be a fundamental change in the nature of the Congregation. Members of the Commission died and were replaced, and all that Paul saw was delay after delay. Finally, in March 1746 he was able to write:

"Thanks be to God, on Monday of Passion week, the twenty-eighth of this month, the day on which the holy Gospel says 'If anyone thirst, let him come to me and drink etc.,' the Vicar of Jesus Christ put his own signature to the Brief[14] confirming our holy Rule; he wrote 'Placet Prospero' [it pleases Prospero], which is the Holy Father's baptismal name."

Crucially the section on Poverty in the Rule had not been touched, but a small number of changes had been incorporated. So any community with more than twelve members would be exempt from the jurisdiction of the Bishop regarding the internal running of the house. Paul

---

[14] *A particular form of document issued by the Vatican.*

had hoped to have the Congregation approved as an Order with solemn vows[15], instead of the simple vows which were taken by his Religious at the time. This would have given fuller exemption from episcopal control, and more freedom with regard to ordination to the priesthood. It would also have made it easier to found a community of contemplative nuns[16], an idea Paul had had for some years. Nevertheless, the Apostolic Brief was a big step forward and gave greater stability to the Congregation of the Passion.

From the beginning Paul had been seen to be the Founder and the creator of the three communities, but with the solemn approval of the Rule it became necessary to hold a General Chapter to elect a Superior. Hardly surprising then that in May 1746 Paul was elected Superior General.

---

[15] *Public vows pronounced in a religious order and recognized as such by the Church. The term has become technical since the recognition of simple but public vows in religious congregations. In practice, a solemn vow of poverty means the actual renunciation of ownership and not merely the independent use of material possessions; and a solemn vow of chastity invalidates attempted marriage.*

[16] *Nuns, as opposed to Religious Sisters, generally are enclosed contemplatives, i.e. they usually live their Religious Life within the confines of their monastery.*

CHAPTER 6

NEW FOUNDATIONS AND FOREIGN MISSIONS

Eighteen postulants[17] entered the Congregation between 1746 and 1747. Vetralla and Soriano had to be extended, but Paul knew he would need to establish new communities. He looked at various possibilities around Rome, but the next Retreat was at Ceccano, which was within the Papal States. A church and hermitage already existed there, but in a very run down state, and situated a few miles out of the town. Tommaso Struzzieri, and Paul's brother Antonio, were sent to Ceccano to prepare for the foundation; the only problem was these two missionaries were frequently away preaching in the surrounding neighbourhood. Paul had hoped that the new community could move in for the feast of the Presentation on 21 November; Tommaso had warned that there was still too much to do and said to delay the move.

In January 1748, after taking a week to travel from Soriano accompanied by Paul, the members of the new

[17] *A candidate seeking admission to a Religious Order.*

community arrived: a priest, two deacons, two sub-deacons and two lay brothers. Despite a very cold and wet journey they received a warm welcome from the Bishop and local people of Ceccano.

The next morning Paul and nine Religious set out for the Retreat accompanied by the Bishop, the clergy and the townspeople; they walked in bare feet through heavy snow. When Paul saw the site he was so disappointed he wanted to turn back, believing that its location was totally inappropriate as it was in the shade of the mountains. The group went on and Paul said the first Mass there, during which he received great consolation, and later confirmed the establishment of the Retreat there, adding that great saints would live there.

As the young Congregation grew, so too did opposition, especially from the mendicant Orders[18]. A proposed foundation in Rome was blocked by the canons of St. Peter's, claiming that the church on the new site was theirs. On a more positive note Tommaso Struzzieri

---

[18] Mendicants were members of any of several Roman Catholic religious orders who assumes a vow of poverty and supports themselves by work and charitable contributions. The main mendicant orders surviving today are the Dominicans, Franciscans, Augustinians, Capuchins and Carmelites.

had received a request from the Bishop of Terracina asking for a Passionist foundation in his diocese. Paul had also been invited to Rome to discuss possible future developments. While there he had a meeting with the Pope who showed great interest in the Retreat at Ceccano. As he left the papal audience Paul was told that a group of Franciscan Friars Minor who opposed the foundation at Ceccano, were also trying to see the Pope, and wanted to present him with a petition against the foundation. The Capuchins also complained to the local Bishop about the Passionists.

In the meantime, Paul was involved in negotiations with the Bishop of Terracina about the new community. Opposition was growing, but the Bishop, who was a Carmelite, wrote to Paul saying opposition was now coming primarily from the Franciscans and Augustinians who feared the Passionists would reduce the income of the other Orders. Paul replied: "As far as I know it is the Capuchins who have stirred up the others, but since I hope they are acting from good intentions, I look on them with particular affection as instruments of the Divine Will, in relation to which I see these events."

While the many negotiations and consultations took place to firmly establish and develop the Congregation,

Paul continued to develop his own prayer life. He did have a spiritual director, but it was clear that Paul's experiences in prayer were very different to the experience of most other people. He often struggled to describe what was happening in his prayer, feeling that the experience went well beyond anything words could describe. Discovering the writings of the German Dominican Johannes Tauler, Paul felt he had encountered a kindred spirit, especially as Tauler wrote about the interior life of the spirit.

Probably due to the opposition of the mendicant Orders in July 1748 the Apostolic Chamber, an office in the Vatican responsible for administering the Papal States, decreed that all building work in progress at the new Passionist foundations was to stop, and what had already been built was to be demolished. The decree was read in the main square at Ceccano; Paul did not hesitate in ordering the community back to Vetralla, but the people would not let them go. Some Friars also sent their most famous member, St. Leonard of Port Maurice, to speak to the Pope against the Passionists. Leonard was a close friend of Benedict XIV, but afterwards regretted what he had done.

In places where the Passionists had communities the town councils wrote to the Apostolic Chamber to protest. In a sense Paul stayed out of the disputes and the politics, simply starting a campaign of prayer within the Congregation. At the same time, he was not passive, but worked hard producing documents defending the Passionists, relying heavily on the legal training of Tommaso Struzzieri.

A commission of Cardinals studied the situation, and in April 1750 gave a decision in favour of the Passionists. The Pope had challenged the opponents of the Passionists, asking them: "Do you want to destroy what we ourselves have built?" Three building programmes were resumed: at Ceccano, Terracina and Paliano, south of Rome; there were now sixty Passionists. Paul and Tommaso Struzzieri were invited by the Pope to preach their first mission in Rome; the Pope and several Cardinals attended the mission.

Now clear of all the trouble with the mendicants Paul was able to devote himself fully to preaching missions, often achieving dramatic results, including the conversion of some notorious characters: robbers and smugglers etc. Not only did Paul reconcile these people, he was often able to plead with the civil authorities for their pardon.

The dominant theme of Paul's preaching was always the love and mercy of God. When he was too old to preach missions he used to say to his missioners, "Let mercy always be uppermost. If I was thirty years younger I would go through the world and preach nothing but the Mercy of God." In the confessional he was the personification of mercy and patience.

His deep sense of unworthiness and incompetence made him reluctant to undertake spiritual direction, but as others did not share his opinion of himself, his correspondence grew steadily. Paul wrote several tens of thousands of letters of spiritual direction; well over 2000 still exist.

In 1758 a Retreat was established at Monte Cavo in the diocese of Frascati. There had been a monastery there but it was long abandoned, and sixteen years earlier Paul had considered it to be a suitable place for a Retreat. It was very dilapidated and renovation was possible only in 1770 due to a donation from the Bishop of Frascati, Henry Stuart, the Cardinal Duke of York! Benedict XIV died in 1758 and was succeeded by a close friend of Paul, the Bishop of Padua who took the name Clement XIII.

With the election of the Clement XIII Paul decided to ask for the establishment of the Passionists as an Order with solemn vows; he also wanted a foundation in Rome. He was told that the requests were difficult but it would help if he himself went to Rome. The Pope was open to the proposals, but had to establish a commission of Cardinals to investigate the matters. Wishing to ensure a suitable outcome the Pope had to wait until 1760 before he could appoint Cardinals who would support the Passionists.

The Rule envisaged Passionists working on the foreign missions, and the first place Paul was asked to send men to was Mossul, in modern day Iraq, on the bank of the river Tigris, across from the ancient city of Nineveh. Paul eventually had to refuse the request due to the death of three religious at Vetralla in 1759 – their deaths caused by drinking wine which was contaminated with poison used to treat the wooden wine barrels. Paul never saw a foreign mission opened, and shortly after his death the French Ambassador blocked a mission to Peking, not wanting to have Italian missionaries in China. Only in 1782 was the first foreign mission opened in Bulgaria.

The papal commission met for its final meeting in November 1760. It decided nothing should be changed for the time being. Apparently the Cardinals wanted to grant the petition, but turned it down for two reasons. The first was the austerity of the Rule, and again the proposal was made that at least the student house should have a stable income; Paul strenuously opposed this and said he would prefer to see the petition entirely rejected "rather than remove this strong wall of holy poverty." The second reason was a major shock for Paul: some of his own religious had written asking for the petition to be rejected, on the basis the Rule was too severe!

Paul was bitterly disappointed by this, and was clearly shocked that some religious had not been open with him, and had actually plotted behind his back. On returning to Vetralla he wrote to the whole Congregation announcing the refusal "for the time being" of the petition. He had prayed to understand the decision and felt able to explain the decision:

"Because our Congregation has fallen from its first observance and fervour; that earlier fraternal charity is no longer that blind obedience, that true holy humility: fervour is little less than extinguished as much by night as by day, there is a great triumph of laziness in the exercises prescribed by the Rule, there is the greatest tepidity in rising to praise God in choir by night and day, mental prayer is full of drowsiness and lack of attentiveness of mind, and there is little or no reverence for the presence of God. There is a noticeable absence of decorum,which indicates a lack of faith and interior reverence."

The decision of the Cardinals to refuse "for the time being" is presented by Paul as an invitation to inner conversion by each religious. The Retreat of the Presentation on Monte Argentario was not a healthy place for novices due to being exposed to the sirocco[19], and also being situated above the stagnant water of the lagoon at Orbetello, a breeding ground for mosquitos. In 1753 Paul decided to build a Retreat, dedicated to St. Joseph, in a much better location, and this would be the noviciate house. Years of negotiation, seeking permissions, raising funds followed and the building work, carried out by the skilled Brothers, was slow. Finally, in 1761 the new noviciate was opened, as Paul wrote:

"The Retreat has been founded to serve as a noviciate and to be a seedbed of saints to provide the Congregation with stalwart and competent men, who will be intimately united with God by charity, to work for the salvation of

---

[19] *Mediterranean wind that comes from the Sahara and can reach hurricane speeds in North Africa and Southern Europe, especially during the summer season.*

souls by being resounding trumpets of the Holy Spirit, to proclaim to all the sufferings of Jesus Christ – the most efficacious means for the destruction of sin – and to urge souls to perfection."

In 1764 Tommaso Struzzieri was appointed a Bishop – an honour for the Congregation, but a major blow for Paul, losing his trusted and capable adviser. The following year John Baptist died, and with his death Paul lost his spiritual director and adviser.

CHAPTER 7

FINAL APPROVAL

For a long time, Paul had wanted a Passionist community to be based in Rome. Several locations were considered before finally, with the help of some generous benefactors, a house was bought from the Jesuits. The Hospice of the Crucified, situated between the Colosseum and the Basilica of St. John Lateran, was opened in early 1767. At the age of 73 Paul wrote to a Carmelite nun:

"In a few days' time, God willing, I will be leaving for a last visit to our Retreats in Campagna and Marittima [the provinces south of Rome], as it is more than fourteen years since I have been there. I am going so as to embrace for the last time my brethren and sons, to whom I will also give a retreat to encourage them to be holy; then, if God gives me life, I will return here to Sant' Angelo, Vetralla, to spend my last days. It is a long, hard journey, and I am a decrepit old man in poor health; I ask for your prayers."

Paul was not exaggerating about his health and frailty; he was now very limited in his ability to walk any distance at all. Consequently, he was forced to travel by carriage. First he visited Monte Cavo in the Alban Hills, before going to the Retreat at Terracina. Due to severe winter weather he remained there for several months before finally travelling to Falvaterra near the Kingdom of Naples. Paul's reputation for holiness was now well established, many people thought of him as a saint. Journeying on to Ceccano people lined the streets to see him and receive his blessing. It was claimed that in earlier years Paul had performed miracles, and now so many people wished to see him that the authorities had to provide an armed escort to protect him. It was reported that so many people cut pieces off his mantle (a type of cloak used as both a coat and a blanket) that he had to be given a new one, before he set off for the Retreat at Paliano, the last Retreat he was to visit.

Returning to Rome, Paul stopped in the Hospice of the Crucified, and from there went to visit the Pope. Whilst staying at the hospice he was visited by a number of Cardinals, and the whole community thought he was close to death, but he made a remarkable recovery, followed by a prolonged period of rest.

While Paul was trying to grow and develop the Congregation, the Jesuits were experiencing persecution from both civil and religious quarters. A number of

European monarchs formed an alliance and tried to force Pope Clement XIII to suppress the Jesuits. He refused and called on a number of Cardinals to formulate a reply to the monarchs. The night before the Cardinals were to meet, the Pope suffered a major stroke and died.

With the death of the Pope Paul had lost a good friend and protector of more than thirty years. Clement had worked from the beginning to have the Rule approved, and had also laboured for the young Congregation to have solemn vows. The conclave to elect the new Pope lasted three months and was dominated by the question of suppressing the Jesuits.

The General Chapter opened in Vetralla in May 1769. Twelve Retreats now formed the Congregation, and in view of his age and infirmity Paul hoped to relinquish the post of Superior General. The Chapter re-elected Paul unanimously. Immediately Paul started to revise the Rule and was soon able to present it to the newly elected Clement XIV, asking him for confirmation and approval of the Rule.

Providentially the Pope lost the actual petition, but from their conversation Paul realised that Pope Clement was willing to do whatever he could to help the Passionists. He prepared a new petition and asked for a lot more, including the approval of the Passionists as a Congregation with Simple Vows, but having the same privileges as Orders with Solemn Vows. Furthermore, he asked for the right to collect donations in any diocese with the Bishop's consent – without having to seek the consent of the mendicant Orders.

Two Monsignors, friends of Paul, worked closely with him, and completed examining the Rule. At the same time Paul was asked to preach a mission in Rome. He excused himself on the grounds of poor health, adding also that he was deaf. The Cardinal Vicar of Rome, who had made the original request replied: "What matters is that the people who come to you are not deaf; your voice sounds fine to me."

Paul then objected to the size of the church chosen for the mission, saying that as he had not preached a mission in five years a smaller church would have to be found. He suggested a tiny church by the River Tiber, used almost exclusively by poor shepherds, fishermen and domestic servants. Because the Cardinal anticipated a large crowd they had to compromise and agreed to use Santa Maria in Trastevere. A few days before the mission was to begin, Paul had a severe attack of malaria and was not able to preach on the first few days of the mission. Paul's first biographer, St. Vincent Mary Strambi, described what happened:

"As soon as he was able to mount the platform[20], he went to take part in the mission, moved by a strong desire to announce the truths of the faith to the people of Rome... There was a great crowd of people of every rank and class, including among them religious, secular priests, prelates, cardinals and the foremost nobles of Rome, and great was the fruit produced; because the venerable servant of God, with true apostolic freedom, without a shadow of human respect, and moved by zeal for the glory of God, inveighed vigorously against the vices and abuses which govern people. That huge audience could be seen in complete silence listening with full attention to the zealous missionary, and when he expressed his innermost feelings, especially in meditating on the Passion of Jesus Christ, they were filled with tenderness of heart. To tell the truth, it was enough to see the venerable old man still recovering from his illness so weak that, to climb the few steps to the platform, he needed the help of several people, some taking him by the hand and others lifting him under the

---

[20] *Passionist missions were often preached not from pulpits but from a series of boards laid out to form a much larger platform, on which would be placed a large crucifix and provide sufficient space for the missioner to stand and move around on.*

arms; when he had reached the platform, he would stand up straight, leaning on his staff, his feet bare, his head uncovered. Then he would begin to preach, doing so with such liveliness, energy and power in his voice that it seemed as if there was nothing wrong with him, so strong was his desire for the salvation of souls."

On the last day of the mission, not only was the Basilica packed, but the great piazza in front was filled with people who could not get in. It was reported that at least another two thousand people were turned away from the piazza as it was so full.

Pope Clement granted everything Paul had requested in his petition, however, Paul noticed that an addition had been made concerning gifts other than money. Paul said this was contrary to the Rule and against the Congregation's understanding of poverty. He also objected to the proposal that a Religious could be dismissed from the Order if they were no longer able to live according to the Rule. He agreed that those who were persistently negligent could be dismissed, but he also argued that individuals should not be dismissed on the grounds of ill health or disability, this, he said, "would not be in keeping with Christian charity, since they have served the Congregation when they were able to do so."

At the end of October Paul visited the Pope in his bedroom, which he described as the room of a poor Religious. The Pope gave him the final text of the Bull[21], and told Paul to take it to the Cardinal to have it copied onto parchment. The Bull "Supremi Apostolatus" was signed on 16 November 1769. The Passionists were now recognised as a Congregation of Pontifical Right, exempt from the jurisdiction of local Bishops. This document made legal history as it was the first time that a Congregation with simple vows was given all the rights and privileges of Orders with solemn vows. Paul had wanted the stability and apostolic freedom of an Order, without taking solemn vows, as this would have necessitated changes in the Rule with regard to Poverty. Clement XIV provided a solution by creating a new category of religious community in which to place the Congregation.

---

[21] *A public decree or charter issued by the Pope.*

CHAPTER 8

FINAL YEARS

Paul felt he had fulfilled his life's work: the Congregation was established and growing steadily, and the Rule had been enhanced and approved. He felt it was time to return to Vetralla and prepare for his death. Pope Clement XIV asked him to remain in Rome, rather than return to Vetralla, and promised to find a church and monastery which would be suitable as a Passionist Retreat.

In March 1770 Paul visited the Pope and told him he was going to visit the Retreats to the north of Rome; he also mentioned a project he had been thinking about for thirty-five years, namely founding a monastery of Passionist contemplative nuns. Already he was aware of a number of women who could form such a community. Building work had started on a monastery for nuns in 1759, but Paul had stopped the work as he believed it would be best to wait until the men's Congregation had been approved.

Now that "Supremi Apostolatus" had been published, Paul asked the Pope to approve a Rule for contemplative nuns, and also permit the opening of a monastery for them. The Pope was pleased with the proposal and said he would approve the Rule. Paul went to Tarquinia where he inspected the building work which had already been done, and while there met one of his benefactors who had three sisters who were Benedictine nuns – Paul had directed one of these over many years, and had chosen her to be the first leader of the new community.

Eventually arriving back at Monte Argentario Paul was able to take some rest, until he was asked to return to Rome as quickly as possible. During the summer months he worked on the Rule for the Passionist nuns. To a large extent it was based on the Rule for the men; for the part dealing with the enclosure (the area of the monastery exclusively for the use of the women) Paul drew on the Constitutions of the Visitation nuns who had been founded by St. Francis de Sales. Even though Paul envisaged the nuns to be contemplatives, he also felt that they could be apostolic, and described how the nuns could give retreats to women, teach catechism to young girls, and instruct females on how to meditate on the Passion.

The two priests appointed to examine the Rule wanted to remove these apostolic elements, but Paul would not agree as he saw this as an expression of the specific nature of the Congregation. The Rule for the Passionist nuns was approved in September 1770, but building work on the monastery at Tarquinia would not be completed for another six months. Yet again Paul was struck with fever which persisted for two full months. Several times he was thought to be close to death and received the Last Sacraments. Pope Clement sent word "We do not want Fr. Paul to die yet." Paul accepted the Pope's message and prayed for his life to be lengthened. From that moment he began to recover.

An extraordinary episode happened at this point in the story of the nuns. A very wealthy Princess, who was a widow and very religious, thought of entering the monastery at Tarquinia. She wrote to the Pope for advice, and he replied that not only should she enter, but at the same time she should be the Superior of the community – maybe the Pope thought her wealth would enable the building work to be completed more rapidly. When the time came for the opening of the monastery the Princess did not appear, and the women who were to form the new community were unable to receive the black habit of the Passionists. Paul was given permission to give the habit to the postulants, and two weeks later the Princess arrived. But two weeks after that she wrote to the Pope saying she wished to leave, apparently the life was too severe; she left in June 1771 before entering a Franciscan monastery, remaining there twenty-five years until her death. In May 1772 the Passionist nuns, who now had eleven members, took their vows, including the distinctive fourth vow to promote the memory of the Passion.

On the international scene the governments of Spain, Portugal, France and Naples were exerting great pressure on the Pope to suppress the Jesuits. This was not a small internal ecclesiastical problem, for it involved most of the major political powers in Europe. The Pope was over a barrel and all he could do was play for time; he came up with various compromises, but these were all rejected by the civil powers. The politicking became so brutal that a threat was made by national governments to suppress all Religious Orders.

Clement XIV persisted in delaying the suppression of the Jesuits, but was finally forced to sign the documentation in July 1773. The Superior General of the Jesuits was arrested and eventually imprisoned in Castel Sant' Angelo where he was totally isolated, fed on half rations, and died after two years. With the suppression of the Jesuits several of their churches in Rome were offered to other Religious Orders. Paul asked the Pope for the gift of Saints John and Paul on the Coelian Hill, a little bit further away from the centre of Rome, and looking over the Colosseum.

In August 1773 Paul was told the Passionists could take over Saints John and Paul – he already had a group of thirty priests, Brothers and students ready to move in. Unfortunately, the Vincentians, who had possession of the monastery, were unwilling to move out even though they were offered a much better church and monastery. They made demands for various payments, and negotiations dragged on. The Pope got fed up and offered Paul an alternative monastery, but Paul felt that the original offer was better suited to the Passionist ideal of the solitary life. Finally, the negotiations were completed and the Passionists took possession of Saints John and Paul.

Paul was now almost eighty years old and Saints John and Paul was the last Retreat he founded. Immediately after the day of their arrival the community began to live the full Religious Life. In the following months Paul had a number of meetings with the Pope who was still deeply disturbed by his suppression of the Jesuits. In these meetings, sometimes lasting a couple of hours, Paul was able to console Pope Clement. Nevertheless, Clement lived in fear of being poisoned or assassinated; in September 1774 Pope Clement XIV died. Paul felt, once again that not only the Congregation, but he personally, had lost a great friend. Clement's papacy was marked by instability and turmoil, primarily due to the question of the suppression of the Jesuits. In marked contrast the Passionists remembered Clement as the Pope who helped them most and gave them stability.

Clement's successor was Pope Pius VI, who two weeks after his election visited Saints John and Paul, solely to meet Paul. Despite now being bed ridden Paul decided to revise the Rule, and planned to present it to the new Pope for confirmation. The General Chapter began in May 1775, and Paul, despite his protests, was once again unanimously elected General. At the end of the Chapter the revised Rule was presented to Pius VI, asking for his approval. Having had the Rule examined yet again, Pius VI approved the revised Rule.

Paul, because of his infirmities, celebrated Mass for the last time on the feast of Corpus Christi in June 1775. At the end of August, knowing he was about to die, he received the last rites of the Church and summoned the community to his bedside. He told them:

"Before anything else I recommend to your attention the observance of that most holy reminder given by Jesus Christ to his disciples: 'By this will all know that you are my disciples, if you have love for one another.' This, dearest brothers, is what I desire with all the affection of my poor heart, both for you who are present and for all the others who are now wearing this habit of penance and mourning in memory of the Passion and Death of our most loveable divine Redeemer, and equally for all who, by God's mercy, will be called in the future to this little flock of Jesus Christ. In addition, I recommend to all, and especially to those who will hold the office of superior, that there should flourish more and more in the Congregation the spirit of prayer, the spirit of solitude and the spirit of poverty, and you can be sure that if these three things are maintained, the Congregation will shine like the sun in the sight of God and people."

He then asked for prayers for the Pope, and recommended various benefactors and individuals to the Community for prayers, and concluded "My dear Jesus... I commend to you now and for ever the poor Congregation which is the fruit of your Cross, your Passion and your Death."

For more than six weeks Paul lay on his bed unable to move. Bishop Tommaso Struzzieri arrived on 18 October 1775 to see Paul and talked with him a short while. Paul died that afternoon while listening to the Gospel account of the Passion being read.

Following the funeral Pope Pius VI asked for the Cause of Canonisation to be opened; this started fifteen months after Paul's death. St. Vincent Strambi, who had lived in Saints John and Paul with Paul published a popular biography, and Paul of the Cross was canonised on 29 June 1867. Vincent Strambi, conscious of Paul's reputation for being severe, wrote of him: "His virtue was not of the terrible and austere kind, but gentle, courteous and full of sweetness." He continued: "He was full of tenderness, compassion and infinite patience. He avoided the gravity that would repel and cultivated an attractive affability which encouraged sinners to come to him." It was Love that drove Paul backwards and forwards, in and out of his religious communities. Here he contemplated God's love and Our Lord's longing for love, and men's need of that love, and the misery and emptiness of their lives because of their ignorance of that love. Undoubtedly he is more to be admired than imitated. Ordinary mortals can only follow him from afar. His vocation was unique; he commented "All are not led the same way; all do not have the same graces."

CHAPTER 9

THE END - OR - THE BEGINNING

It was to be expected that his spiritual gifts as founder of the Congregation dedicated to the Passion of Christ would lead Paul to a unique relationship with Christ Crucified. Yet even when advanced in holiness he did not begin to enjoy, like some of the saints, a foretaste of the joys of heaven. The great graces he received brought only a deeper appreciation of Christ's suffering.

Also like his Master on Calvary, he experienced a terrifying sense of abandonment by God; and in a mysterious intellectual way, he seemed to participate in Christ's sufferings. He once described his state as "like being in hell." For him this state meant the utter deprivation of all sensible consolation, the black-out of his knowledge of the spiritual life, a sense of total abandonment. He was sorely tempted to despair. Only very occasionally did he enjoy brief intervals of consolation when he seemed to be sheltered from the tempest in the wounds of Christ. It was what he asked for, what he wanted, but that did not make it any easier to bear.

To Paul, Calvary was a mystery of obedience unto death: the greatest demonstration of love, and at the same time the greatest obstacle to faith. If God used the unique event to decide to redeem us, He can use the enigmas of our world today for a divine purpose too, no matter how revolting and meaningless they may seem.

Opposition and disappointment dogged Paul's life to the end, but in his closing years God gave him some great consolations. One was the foundation, after the usual sequence of opposition and setbacks, of the Order of enclosed contemplative Passionist nuns.

At the end of his life St. Paul of the Cross was heard to say that for fifty years he had been praying for the conversion of England. He died in 1775; consequently, as the Order was established in 1725, during all of his Passionist life he must have had this devotion very close to his heart. Often was he heard to murmur: "Ah England, England, let us pray for England." In his thanksgiving after Mass, often he experienced ecstasy, and on one occasion, when he came out of the ecstasy he seemed bewildered. He then, with a smile of happiness on his face, exclaimed: "Where was I just now? I was in spirit in England considering the great martyrs of the time past, and praying to God for that kingdom."

God did not leave him without an answer to that prayer. In prayer Paul was told that at a future date his sons would labour in that country of his dreams. Having celebrated Mass one day, he had a vision which filled him with so much joy that he wept, and he sobbed: "What have I seen! My children in England!" Commenting on this Blessed Dominic Barberi said: "We may presume that some further particulars were communicated to him on that occasion to console him and strengthen his hope for the conversion of this realm, so dear to his heart; however this was, it is quite sure that he went on to the end incessantly praying for the welfare of this country and never could lose sight of it; as he used to say to himself 'It would be impossible for me to abstain from praying for England, because, as soon as I kneel down to pray, England comes before my eyes'."

It would be many years before the vision of Paul of the Cross would be fulfilled. The first realistic moves were made by Father (now Blessed) Dominic Barberi, who claimed that in a vision he was told: "that I was to bring back stray sheep to the true fold. It did not specify to me how, when, where, to whom, – whether infidels, heretics, or bad Catholics – but left a hazy notion in my mind that the mission in store for me would not be amongst Catholics solely. I was astonished at such an announcement, and could not imagine how it could be verified. However, as I felt I could not doubt that the communication came from God, so I could not doubt for an instant that it would be fulfilled."

Dominic (1792 – 1849) was convinced he was called to work in England, but throughout his life he was prevented until 1841 when he went to England and spent the last eight years of his life establishing the Passionist Congregation there. Among those he eventually worked with were Fr. Charles Houben (St. Charles of Mount Argus), Fr. Ignatius Spencer whose Cause for Beatification is currently in Rome, along with Mother Mary Prout the Foundress of the Sisters of the Cross and Passion. These three holy people were clearly fulfilling the vision of St. Paul of the Cross in terms of Passionists working for the conversion of England and the surrounding countries.

THE PASSIONISTS

The Passionist Congregation was founded in Italy in 1720 by St. Paul of the Cross, and brought to England in 1842 by Blessed Dominic Barberi. It is a worldwide Order of priests and brothers who preach the love and suffering of the Crucified Christ.

THE POSTULATOR

For information about favours received through the intercession of Blessed Dominic Barberi or Fr. Ignatius Spencer, please contact the Vice Postulator:

Fr. Ben Lodge CP
St. Joseph's Retreat
Highgate Hill
London
N19 5NE